Sunrise Ruby

poems of reality and hope

by

Karen Warinsky

"We must use time wisely and forever realize that the time is always ripe to do right."
— Nelson Mandela

"The wisest are the most annoyed at the loss of time."
—Dante Alighieri

Acknowledgements

The author wishes to acknowledge the editors of the following publications and online sites in which the following poems appeared:

Blue Heron, Issue 12 Nurturing Hope, Spring, 2021, "I Came to Watch Birds;" *Circumference Poetry Institute*, June 2021, "Forgotten City" and "No Bowling for You," and *Circumference Poetry Institute*, June 2022, "Muon, Like Me," "Nine More," and "The French Club Goes to Chicago;" *Consilience*, Spring 2022, "Footnotes;" *Verse Virtual*, December 2021, "Petroglyph," "Clean Up Crew," and "The Beats Go On."

Published by Human Error Publishing
Paul Richmond
www.humanerrorpublishing.com
paul@humanerrorpublishing.com

ISBN: 978-1-948521-03-1

Cover art by Arden Warinsky
Photo by Janet McDonald

Table of Contents

Getting Here

The Fight

The Balm

~~ Getting Here ~~

Getting Here

By the time you get
here
to this place
desires are still too heavy
and you realize
it may not be possible
in the time
left
after the washing, ironing, shopping,
arranging, sustaining and
dusting,
to get those moments
those quiet, inspired
micro-moments
where ideas can float in
for digestion and you can
shoot them back out
like smart little stars,
shining in a sky of your creation,
background blue,
background black,
there for anyone to look up and see.

It's not a secret once you write it down,
send it around with a keystroke.
Connection becomes real and you see
the proof on the page that
                                    you are here.

Silent Night

Just another Silent Night,
have been many in my life,
since college days where a city of friends
were mine for the taking
as we crammed into dorms, rooming houses,
shabby apartments,
sat cross-legged in a circle on the floor,
counter culture natives
inhaling nature,
exhaling dreams,
pounding out a philosophy
to carry us on.

Later, juggling the act of work, chores,
kids, emergencies,
mine and others,
and running, running, running till
knees protested
and walking became all,
TV and seclusion a blessing.

Now, children are grown,
the job is done and winter weighs heavy by 4 o'clock,
the darkest of the year.
Shells of snow crust everything,
sad cats pace the kitchen
longing for the warm grass,
or to perch on their summer porch,
and I plot my survival strategy
to outlast this world gone viral
with fear and pessimism,
and a realization by some
that we either win this match together
or lose the game.

Civil Disobedience

I named my first bicycle the "Blue Beast"
until I learned to ride.
Used, with thick 3- inch tires
it was true heavy metal
pressing full against my leg
as I readied to ride or whenever I stopped,
challenging me to take control.
This second- hand bike,
procured somewhere by my father,
produced freedom
as I circled the neighborhood for hours.

Riding, I observed other families,
learned their foibles,
sometimes their secrets,
met my friends,
sometimes squabbled,
sometimes got a treat from a beleaguered mom,
and enjoyed myself
but
where the end of Watson Drive went perpendicular to 23
there was a Siren calling.
Odysseus himself could not have resisted.

"Don't cross the hard road," Mom would say,
her southern reference to the two-lane.
"Do not leave Ada-lore Heights!
You don't have my permission to go downtown."

She had made it clear.

But one day, as I stood at that crossroads
realizing she could not see me,
would never know if I left or not
those Greek temptresses whispered in my ear
and I took off.

Coasting down the gentle slope of Main Street,
feet off the pedals,
hair flying wild behind me,
I initiated my first act of
Civil Disobedience.

Beauty Lesson

Busy devout moms went around town on Saturdays,
curlers poking out beneath their scarves,
tied tight on their heads and pinned in place at the temples.
This Saturday sacrament was seen in every shop and store
as the women readied for evening mass,
or for Sunday worship,
and their sacrifice impressed me,
their willingness to be seen in rollers
a serious devotion
as mothers like mine would only leave the house
dry and intact.

Young girls used devices that clipped in place
over rectangles of pink foam, hair coiled like a fishing reel
producing a wide, droopy flip, that flopped in the humidity.

Others snapped rubbery spools around sections of hair
creating rows of painful pink plastic quarters
on their heads,
taking hours to dry.
It took forever and I'd have to sleep with it overnight
to get the desired result.
I would arrange mine so nothing was behind
my 10-year-old neck,
trying to find a comfortable position for sleeping.
Mom convinced me my straight hair would look better
with some curl, so I used this torturous method.
Ladies with bobs simply stuck their ear curls to their cheeks
with Dippity Do and tape,
wincing in pain when they pulled it off.

It was clear these rituals were important.

My mother favored the downtown beauty shop
coming home once a week
in a cloud of Aqua Net or White Rain.
For a while she fancied a "French bun,"

a teased three-scoop cone of hair sitting
eight inches off the top of her head.
Think Bardot. Think Audrey Hepburn.
Think, she worked in a factory.

Caroline Chase, a willowy, silent teenage girl
would float goddess-like along Main Street on Saturdays,
in cut-offs, t shirt and a look of distracted disdain.
I would see her downtown,
me straddling my blue one-speed bike,
standing in front of the Ben Franklin
chomping on candy watching this local star
walk slow on the sidewalk
her hair wound around hollow Coke cans.
So exotic.
Think Cosmopolitan.
Think, she married early.

The checkout lady at the Big Blue lost her eyebrows
replacing them with a most original
carrot-colored marker.
Every time I bought a comic book or a dill pickle,
I studied her brows,
marveling at those burnt-orange arches.

Then I learned my first beauty lesson
the summer the pool opened
and we had to wear swimming caps,
hiding our hair,
showing only our little fleshy faces,
our cute, shiny braids tucked up under
puckered rubber caps
making us look like those Onion head dolls
so popular back then,
the insides of the caps smelling like motor oil.
That's when I realized the worth of my hair,
and began to understand
what all the furor was about.

A Boy in Sixth Grade

Dirt smears on cheeks, under nails,
muddy patch in the grassless yard
chained dogs cold and unfed
junk cars
broken toys out in four seasons.

Tatty coat
natty clothes
greasy hair
salty smell of urine
keeping other kids away
no one at recess, no one at lunch.

Slow to answer,
the teacher waits for the sum
the correct response
the line to be read
and I would pray
he would get the answer
and commute his sentence.

Calling Names

Our little farm town
so humble and sweet,
tidy shops lining Main Street,
sidewalk sale days in summer,
the carnival in June,
friendly neighbors.

But who was the little girl
with only three dresses in her closet?
I went to her house once,
her bedroom bare and cold
no rug on the floor,
no pictures on the wall
the dresses hanging lettuce limp.

And what happened to Libby Baines,
a Tennessee transplant with a worn winter coat
and an accent everyone taunted.
Dark-headed and pale
she walked with me to choir practice,
her gloveless fingers red raw in the November air.
She was gone by Spring.

What became of feeble Teddy Beckler,
a simpleton who wandered the town,
smiling and chatty,
friendly as a pup, just hanging out at the Big Blue,
sometimes dangling his long legs
off the hood of that abandoned car
in the lot next to his mother's shack?
What was their fate?

How was I spared?
Why was I so lucky
never to be called mean names?

Hometown Scenes

I

Before bomb threats became a thing
there was Dewey.
That boy was crazy,
but didn't look it.
Looked more like a young accountant
in the high school hallways;
hair combed, nice tie, sweater vest.

He called in a bomb threat--then told everyone about it;
I remember being grateful to be out on the sidewalk
that pretty spring day,
not especially worried,
knowing it couldn't possibly be real,
just glad to have a delay taking my history final.
This was 1972, before it really became a fad
to call one in on a day when
there was a big test
or to rattle the general population.

Then there was the time he killed a chicken
at the Homecoming pep rally.
The signs taped to the windows
of the blue Volkswagon said,
"Huck the Fawks." and kids went wild
as the jocks drove that car into the gym.
The principal let them
take the gymnasium doors off to do it.
I doubt he knew about the signs
or the chicken,
unwitting stand-in symbol for our rival team.

Poor Dewey.

He just got too excited and he wrung that chicken's neck.
At least that's what they told me.
I was in the pep band, and didn't see it,
but I heard the crowd roar.

II

Sweet Sugar Sam looked like a character from Dune,
obese with a jeweler's eye piece affixed to one lens
of his black rimmed glasses,
suspenders holding up size 44 polyester pants,
inch thick glasses
magnifying every move,
every strand of hair on a young girl's head.
He owned the joint where you could
get a syrupy Green River for 30 cents,
sit for an hour with your friends at the counter,
while faded photos in black and white
of sports teams 20 years gone
looked down upon you,
ghostly teens looking earnest and proud
hanging over our heads as we sipped our sodas,
their bodies leaning away from the wall in their frames,
black wires pulling on ancient nails,
their youth already evaporated like the dry ice
keeping things cool in the giant freezer.

Was he a coach back then?

When I was 16 my girlfriends worked there in the summer;
said the job included going to his house,
making up the bed, sweeping up the kitchen,
listening to lewd remarks and dodging those old hands.
But hey, it paid $3.00 an hour,
so who cared?

III

I used to time it so I would be in the hallway
when you walked by between classes.
Your open flannel shirt would fly out
around your t-shirt tucked tight
inside those snug, worn jeans.
Sometimes our arms would touch,
and on the best days
you would look at me
and smile.

Years later you sold farm equipment,
were divorced and pudgy.
Was that disappointment I felt, or relief?

The Spoils of Progress

I

Her survival skills included
bargain hunting,
accessorizing,
and 30-minute recipes.
She could adjust the Buick's carburetor
and didn't take crap off
surly clerks and salesmen.

She grew rose bushes, not vegetables,
mended, but didn't sew,
leaned on modern conveniences;
processed food,
packaged desserts,
Aqua Net for her hair,
Raid for the bugs.
She questioned nothing,
read no labels,
poured Red Dye #6 into the cake frosting
and put # 12 on her lips.
That was my mom,
same as most moms in my town,
cooking supper in Teflon and aluminum,
buying us Captain Crunch for breakfast,
telling us to be home by dark.

II

Stunned by an offering of raw vegetables at a party,
scared of the hippies in our apartment house
who kept offering me nuts and granola,
my awakening was slow,
finally finding the path to the herbs and fibers,
the hidden histories,
the lost knowledge,

the inner self,
the ways of natives,
trying to rectify my past
hanging from the neck of all the pasts,
and give a push forward.

Laugh

Grandpa swore nearly every other word,
a lifetime of gruff
built up by years of horse training and railroading,
of keeping kids in line with a belt
and a stern voice.

"Howdy Pardner," or "Hey Hot Shot,"
was all I ever got from him
a friendly acknowledgment
but it was Grandma who knew me,
who chuckled with me over the details of my young life.

"This is a God-damned nice church," he said,
sitting with my mother waiting to hear me
sing in the children's choir.
Mom exhaled a mortified rebuke;
"Dad, keep your voice down!"
"Damn nice," he added.

Like I said, he swore a lot.

One night after supper
as the adults sat on the porch in the thick summer air
sipping tea and swatting flies,
we stayed inside
Grandma and me
behind the screen door,
counting how many times he said, "God-damn."
By number 13 we were crying,
howled when he leaned toward the door,
asked,
"What the Sam-hell's going on in there?"
Age ten, unable to breathe, holding my sides,
rolling on the floor
as you shook in your chair
your smoker's cough taking your air,
that's my favorite memory of you.

Austin

No real inclination to go to Austin
though I hear it's quite a scene,
music pouring from the doors of bars,
cold beer and friendly folk.
But I would wait again on the sidewalk
by the dime store
for Susie and Shell
so we could blow our allowance
on some Chiclets and Pixie Stix.

Haven't ever hankered to see Berlin,
ride its modern subway,
go to mod millennial night clubs,
but it would be special to sit again
at the end of Grandma's yard,
feet plashing in the ditch after a summer storm,
eyes on the old widow woman across the street
sitting alone on her porch in her prairie bonnet.

Didn't feel I missed much
when the train blew past Albany,
but what wouldn't I give to walk up your porch steps,
hear you holler for me to come in,
look into the smile that was your hazel blue eyes?

The French Club goes to Chicago

This is for Jim,
a 20-something waiter
at the fancy French restaurant
Miss Larkin took us to in "the city,"
a busload of boisterous school girls
feeling every bit of 16,
bold after viewing *Claire's Knee*.

His funky round glasses
framed an alert look;
he knew the power of women,
observed us warily as we flirted and sassed
beyond Miss Larkin's reach,
the other girls trapped by her presence
at their end of the table.

Poor Jim!
He offered us tangerines
after the meal
which we took like treasure.
Later, some girls threw them out the bus windows
captive to an inexpressible wildness.

And this is for the business man I saw
as he walked along Wacker Drive at 5 p.m.,
his work day done,
the bus taking us back to our country town,
our waiting parents.
He looked up, adjusting his neck scarf,
our eyes met and I swear we had a moment,
each wondering about the other's life,
he, having no idea about Jim, or Miss Larkin,
and me, holding my orange
like a tiny globe.

Like Bill Murray, the lark
(After The Song of the Lark by Jules Breton)

Yes, it was the main thing I noticed
in the foyer of the Chicago Art Museum,
a school kid off the bus
ready for my Windy City field trip.

She stands, placid,
contemplative
head up, body still
listening,
and the title of Breton's painting
tells us
it is a lark she hears.

This is the print I took home that day,
spending nearly all I had
to buy the marigold sky,
pink halo sun,
dawn's sure promise,
the girl's poise.

In his story
Murray was dejected,
walking right off the stage in the middle of the play,
humiliated by his terrible performance.
Thinking he'd never be an actor,
ready to court death, he walked blind for miles
through the south side,
till he found himself at the art museum.
Entering, he saw the painting,
the morning and the girl listening to the lark,
and her hope
made him live another day.

Muon, Like Me

I did not always behave as predicted,
did not conform to the Standard Model
distressing my parents
wobbling about like that tiny muon,
reacting to unseen forces.

Scientists are stirred on their grand quest
to understand this four-letter word,
this muon,
along with other quivers, quavers and quarks
and dark matter
(they are pulled into that quite completely),
troubled by why there is matter at all,
unable to take a native approach,
just be grateful and give thanks.

My childhood fights were against wearing
beautiful dresses of scratchy cloth,
staying in the yard,
early bedtimes.
Youthful explorations involved having a good time,
surviving on a modest salary,
getting somewhere in a career,
and seeking that other four-letter-word,
love
which, like the muon,
is heavy and unstable,
decaying rapidly.

The muon's "magnetic moments"
fill researchers with awe;
they suspect
it can connect
with a host of the universe's potential,
because joining with just one other
is too limiting for love,
too limiting for creation,

and this news brings me relief
as I am ready to stretch out,
increase my capacity
like this newfound cosmic crumb.

Two of the Three Times
I Could Have Been Raped

I

Walking into a bedroom
at a college house party
fetching my coat
you ambushed me,
closed the door,
stood and stared
the trap inside your eyes.

You looked desperate, wild,
but I wasn't afraid,
knew all I had to do was wait.
Either someone would come in
or we could keep moving back and forth,
the bed between us,
never changing sides.

II

Her name was also Karen.
She was pregnant.
We worked together.
I was new to town
excited with my first real job.
Taking the trash out behind my apartment house,
a man working on his truck said hello.
We chatted.
Turned out he was her husband.
Now I had two friends.
He asked if I'd seen Sibley Park.
I had not and so I climbed into
his now repaired truck ready for
a quick tour,
but once in the park
he pulled into a grove of trees,

turned off the engine,
and lunged.
What made him stop?
My complete horror or
his embarrassment
at mistaking friendliness
for a come on?

Pushing my body hard against the door
as if the metal could protect me
as if I could push through to the other side,
we drove back in silence.

I lived there another year.
I never saw him again.
I didn't tell anyone.

Karen had her baby.

Broken Dolls

Akimbo, they sit.
Slumped in chairs too big
or too small, some strapped in,
some leaning 90 degrees,
quizzical expressions with heads tilted
like the RCA dog,
waiting for an answer to a question.
Clothing askew, pant legs up showing skin
between the ankle and the knee, disarming disarray.

Give it an extra spray on top,
gotta look good for tonight.
Lipstick smeared? No. Seams straight? Good.
Slip showing? No slip.
Do you like these shoes with this skirt?

They lay in darkened rooms with rumpled covers,
fuzzy socks with grip strip bottoms on helpless feet,
hands clutching Kleenex
repeating useless motions, rubbing buttons,
twirling rings,
hands that were once useful, needed.

Grab that dough...don't handle it too much!
Push it flat on that dusting of flour. Roll it gently
out from the center! Not too thin!

They wait, anxious for interaction,
for a son or daughter, a nurse,
a visitor from the outside to bring them
a message for their bottle.
This is life's end. Lingering, undignified,
questions in their eyes that tea parties
and indoctrination cannot answer.

My Baby Now

She is my baby now.
Didn't see this coming.
Really should have,
runs in the family,
crazed, demented women
needing care from angry, reluctant daughters.

Always tried to make me promise
she'd never be put in a nursing home.
Plead with me
her eyes full of helplessness and blame.
Gelatinous brown eyes magnified
through her thick lenses,
eyes that tried to burn a path of shame
through my heart, sending a warning.

What was I to say?
All I could say was nothing.
I did that a lot.

"I will do my best," I said.
I never promised.
I also never told her the truth,
that it was wrong of her to ask such a thing,
a thing only the very rich or retired can do,
become a 24 hour a day caregiver.

"Give up all you have to care for me!"

Full time, around the clock,
24 hours a day with a woman
I struggled with my entire life?
A woman who found ways to criticize most things
I did; the way I wiped a dish dry,
placed a magazine on a table,
the cut of my hair,
a woman skilled at projecting

her own fears onto me.

I had spent a lifetime peeling off her notions.
Didn't she know what she was asking?

I knew what would truly satisfy her
was if I crawled into the bed with her,
put my things in the dresser
and called for the nurse.
She wanted me as a shadow.
She always wanted my shadow.
I yanked it back from her multiple times,
and finally, like Wendy in the tale,
I sewed the stolen shadow back on myself
and left the house.

But she is my baby now.

Now I hold her good hand,
put polish on the nails,
pick out her clothing, help feed her meals,
make sure she is treated right.
The past cannot be addressed,
avoided all those years
to keep the peace, keep it nice.
I have made the good outweigh the bad;
forced the good to count for more,
because she is my baby now.

The Dermatologist Looks at Death

This time we have to use a wheelchair,
he cannot make more than three or four feet
before needing to sit, to rest.
When we get to the door at the corridor's end
it's obvious the chair will not go through.
"C'mon dad. Stand up.
Let's just walk to the waiting room first,"
I say in my studied, steady voice,
the voice I once used with my children
when they were scared or unruly.
Once inside, he is uncomfortable on the exam table.
I adjust head and foot rests till he sits coffin-still,
not quite like he does in his Lazy Boy at home.

The young doctor is kind,
speaks to my father's shadow,
this man who now takes several moments
to come out with an answer,
the man who has been so unhappy
for most of his life.

"How are you today, sir?" the kind doctor asks.

Dad replies he is "a stranger in a strange world,"
bewildering the doctor,
obviously used to more conventional conversation.
"I'm so sorry you feel like that," he finally manages.

I used to be embarrassed
by Dad's sad, obscure remarks
but at this point it is all truth,
and memories of how he'd distress me
in front of my friends
with answers that revealed only defeat
no longer have effect.

Finally, the head doctor arrives

her alarmed eyes and hard face
exude her wonder that I have drug
such a deflated tire of a person into her office,
wasting her time; he is so obviously dying.
Middle aged, this woman must, like me,
see and taste it around her,
smell it in the fallen autumn leaves,
try to distract herself with her busy schedule,
her growing family,
her daily spray of perfume.

Requiem

Of course, I loved you.
Of course, you loved me.
Why did so many things get in the way
of that truth?
Something that should be so simple and clear
deteriorated into a foggy mash of chides,
slights, silences,
untold tales, hurt feelings.
Your constantly hurt feelings.
How did I manage to always hurt your feelings
by being myself?
Coping with your past,
your perceptions honed from real disasters,
I did my best,
but where was the grace and understanding for me
as I tried to navigate my very present life?
Why wasn't there ever room for my sorrows?

Walking back to the good times
got harder every year
as I tried not to step on the cut glass of your pain,
your fragile ego that littered the floor,
exacerbated by the medications;
the Demerol, the Tramadol,
the Extra Strength everything.
You told your tale. I listened for years.
This tale is mine to tell.
But of course, I loved you.

Experience

Watching, listening, learning,
creating,
we are here for the
experience.
Sometimes there is a bonus,
a closeness appears out of nowhere,
or something worked for
turns out good and satisfying.
Understanding emerges after a delve,
or gifted through grace,
and we sit with another piece of the sky, the land,
wind- blown notes coming through like
5-part harmony,
the message crisp, clear, pleasing.

Then, the opposite...
appreciation taught through contrast;
we take a beating,
feel loss,
suffer a consequence,
live through a dry season.

Who named him Experience Allen?
Did she know
he would one day rest in Union, Connecticut,
his stone on a little hilltop cemetery?
Did she know he would make me conjure an image,
put the encounter on paper,
sense his past in my present moment
and marvel at her motherly love?

Time Signature

A trick of the mind
is time,
sometimes so slow
you doodle,
revisit old loves,
let your OCD take over
and count all the squares on the floor,
the stripes on the curtains.

Other times you must

remember
                    to
                              breathe,

roll your shoulders
uncurl your toes
because the stress of the pace of some task
has you clenched,
a fist of flesh
as you race the clock
to meet another deadline.

The time signature of my life plays with me,
sometimes it's a waltz in 4/4,
other times 16th notes are pounded out
on the day's keyboard
and all I can do is whisk the hair out of my face
and try to direct the music.

Hard Reset

Techno jargon makes it clear,
I need a hard reset and a 301 redirect because
there's been a 404 error in my life
and it's time to clear the cache
before I cash out.

Might be good if I could boost my Google,
use some minification,
pull out all the useless, excess stuff,
increase my page load speed.

That would boost my Google for sure.

The self-help world knows
I could use some radical laughter,
because all this thinking about the singularity,
Tyler, and the AI
has put some dark matter clumps in my brain
and I wouldn't want
dark matter hunters poking around in there
with their dark energy
as I contemplate those dancing dragon fossils
found by a Chinese farmer,
a pterosaur in the petrichor,
or while I ponder the Higgs bosun particle,
CRISPR technology and
functional unit organoids.

I want to stay away from the dark mode,
check my modus operandi,
heist my zeitgeist.

We live in a world where a tree is worth more
dead than alive,
same as a whale, a cow,
a man with good insurance.
What are the implications?

I need some Alt text
because I've abandoned my cart
and my cookies are being tracked
somewhere inside my Disaster Recovery Plan
or maybe...

I just need a good plug-in and a hard reset.

Crone

A crone is coming.
She is not so wise as wizened,
not so clever as canny.
No longer 17 inside, but perhaps 50.
Sixty-two is the new 50, she pretends,
but 63 sounds old, and she isn't really down with that.

Some dreams shook hands
while others scattered like balls of mercury
rolling across a linoleum floor.
She saw that once when her mother
dropped the thermometer.
They spent an hour trying to capture the silver droplets,
eventually pushing them into a plastic cup.
The mercury cup was taken to the burn barrel
and blazed away,
though that is dangerous for dreams; deferment and all.

When do you give up on your dreams?
When just moving the body becomes a daily task?
When all the washing and folding and paperwork finally
just takes too damn much time and
you can't fit it all in?
Is that why people become homeless?
Unable to keep up with the demands of their modern life
do the pieces just pull apart one by one till
there's only a suitcase of stuff so heavy
they need a shopping cart to push it around?
Could that happen to her?
How much longer will she fight?
Fight for those remaining dreams?
Fight for some more golden experiences?
She had her turn, she knows, but would still like another,
holding her bowl like Oliver Twist, asking for more.

Black Ibis

The moon was just a sliver that night,
slight light allowing sleep,
not a vivid stream keeping me awake
pondering mysteries and meanings.

The car was moving fast
bird wings beating all around me,
slapping my arms and head.

This large black bird was in the front seat next to me,
beak like a sickle it tried to take the wheel,
drive us off the road.
We struggled together,
and I wondered how I knew
this bird was an Ibis.

I learned the Egyptians
deemed it the bird of wisdom and writing
magic and the moon
symbol of Thoth
god and clarifier.

Just fighting with myself in the end, it seems,
ever torn between my desire for understanding
and time enough to scribble down what's understood.

I Came to Watch Birds

I came to watch birds sit at the feeder,
buzz around the yard.

I came to sip hot coffee,
eat a sweet cookie,
feel the icing melt on my tongue.
I came to smell the sunblock on my skin
charging up from sunrays
after too long a winter.

I came to see that finch,
yellow and in peril
his brightness a curse.
Gingerly taking a seed,
he eats it,
looks around,
charily takes another.

I came to meet you.
We laughed for a time,
and your memory has lingered
for a great many years,
helping me in days of trouble,
blessing me in days of peace.

~~ The Fight ~~

9 minutes, 29 seconds

8 minutes and 46 seconds is Fake News.
It took longer by over minute thirty
to kill George Floyd,
a father, partner,
brother,
beloved son.

It's in the record now.
George Floyd has a Wikipedia page.
Police video made it clear exactly how long it took
for life to be pressed from his body.

Nine minutes, 29 seconds.

He had triumphs, he had trouble.
Not like mine,
different than mine,
but
I also would not last ten minutes with a knee on my neck,
could have met hard consequences
from my own poor decisions
in a system that didn't value me.
Could have wound up in jail trying to get a foothold,
be strong
provide, live wise.

Our signs were wrong that day
as we knelt paying tribute to this stranger,
this dead, unknown man,
but now we know: it was 9 minutes, 29 seconds.

Things Get Lost

Things get lost,
memories fade
too much history to remember—
too many ancient kings, dust entombed cities
battles won and lost and won again,
countries and capitals renamed.

Parchment crumbles
stone cuts soften,
ancestors fall from view.
We forget their names.
Beautiful names
chosen by careful mothers
bestowing benedictions on babies
for a plentiful, happy future.

And so today,
before things get lost
say their names:
Breonna, Philando, Trayvon,
Ahmaud, Atatianna.
Harmonic syllables
rolling out in a cadence of hope
unmet in this world.

Say their names.

Attention Span

Sometimes God seems to have a dad's attention.
You know,
the dad who lets you jump on the couch,
have a sip of beer,
hold an army knife when you're five.
Occasionally this dad is very involved,
angry even,
shouting at you to do better.
Other times he is napping
while you pick on your little brother.

These genocides are ever present, ever growing,
solutions missing from political conversations,
as Rohingya are killed on the roads,
Syrians survive in rubble,
their escaped countrymen lingering in Moira,
a dismal, failed camp on the isle of Lesbos.
American homeless are unwelcome, unwanted,
pressed out of even the dankest cement city corridors,
chased from marshy spaces on the edges of towns,
tents and possessions become fuel for a bonfire.

A mother,
a loving mother,
would not leave her children to wallow and die in distress.
Only an inattentive dad, eyes glued to a ball game,
waiting to see if his pool pick will win.

September Day

Her birthday was September 11th,
but that didn't make her
any nicer of a person.
She used to sit at different lunch tables,
listening,
get as much gossip as she could
and report back to various administrators.
I learned this
through observation and my inner compass,
making sure to fold my thoughts
like a fresh tissue,
keep them in my pocket.

*** *** ***

They arrived at JFK at 12:45 a.m.
The flight had been uneventful but difficult
because they were worried and nervous,
immigrating from Bosnia with their three young children,
the boys ten and six, their daughter, Azra, just eight.
She had her birthday the day before they left,
cried because there would be no party.
That morning as the weary family
settled into the back bedroom of their uncle's house
the first plane hit.

*** *** ***

I knew nothing until about 11 a.m.
because I was writing from home that day,
finishing up a story with a deadline,
so when I finally checked the news
I saw a small photo of a plane
and the name of buildings I didn't know: Twin Towers.

How had I never heard of these buildings?

Just the arc of my life.
Sitting still for a while
my thoughts percolating,
I suddenly went outside, got in the car,
drove to each school
to collect all three children.
At the Middle School
the principal came to the locked door
which was odd
because the front door was never locked
back then,
and he smiled and said,
"They are fine. Everything is fine,"
and acted like I should just leave them there.

"I want them," I said,
and I made him give them to me,
my children,
and I took them home and we sat
in the downstairs family room,
waiting for what was to come next.

*** *** ***

The music parents held their first meeting in September.
This time it was on that day,
and the dad in charge said he'd like to have
a moment of silence for all the victims,
but later I realized the silence wasn't for everyone.
The next year I made sure to add the estimates
of the more than half million dead
Iraqis and Afghanis to our moment.

It was very silent.

Heroes, Too

People heard the blast
ran fast
grabbed children
helped each other outside into the daylight
hugged tight while smoke cleared,
rubbed soot from their eyes.

They searched the rubble,
put out fires,
heard soft cries get fainter
till hope vanished from
certain quarters,
certain corners.

They held the hands of survivors,
of victims,
their own hands,
wrapped arms around their torsos,
swayed back and forth
till hearts beat in a regular rhythm,
their souls finally settling like the dust.

Iraq.
          Afghanistan.

800,000 dead.

How long will it take to read those names?

Battle Ground States

"I am like a ruby held up to the sunrise,
Is it still a stone, or a world made of redness?
It has no resistance to sunlight. The ruby and the sunrise
are one. – Rumi

The heart has rusted
left out in political weather,
damaged from too many battles
too much unrest
too little acceptance.

We face ourselves and choose;
stay and fight or cut and run,
give all for a worthy cause
or hide our treasure,
then forget where its buried.

This nation was sung into consciousness
from the mountains to the prairies, to the oceans
but we do not own the deed;
it belongs to slaughtered natives and slaves,
to the Civil War dead,
to Lincoln sleeping in his tomb,
to innocents bombed in churches, synagogues and temples,
to all who died seeking justice.
They wait for our next move
the weight of their sacrifice pressing our chests.

We live in a battle ground state,
place of flags and separation,
rhetoric and emotion,
and to heal this country's twisted metal heart
we must work alchemy
try to help it shine, like a Sunrise Ruby.

Put Your Flags Away

One comes down, another is created
designed, laid out and sewn.

Flags.

Flags for your rivalries
your misplaced ethnic pride
your turf wars
your teams
your favorite season.

Just get with it.
We all come from Africa.
The heart of humanity is there, some scientists say,
and we traveled
spread ourselves out
in the four directions
creating cultures and chaos in equal parts.
Why post a flag about it?
Plenty to be proud of.
Plenty to be ashamed of.

And here we all sit about to choke together in this
tarnished world
and another flag won't clean the air,
pull plastic from the ocean,
put nutrients back into the land
though you could wipe the kitchen counter with it,
make a little more "counter space" if you get my drift.
Perhaps that's where we have to head,
into the counterspace, the place of subtle forces
opposing Euclid's geometry,
going inward
where we can create and recreate infinitely,
ponder the deep mysteries of life.
We need a new dimension
because this one is too full of flags,
and I want to sit down.

Forgotten City

Life returned
to the stubbled hills
to the ancient stones
though archeologists with lithified hearts bewail:
refugees are moving the rocks!

Who cares about refugees?

Syrians,
pommeled and pounded
for years now
live among the ruins of Byzantine,
ruined themselves.

Nestling against half-walls
rose-pink in the dawn,
they pen their animals,
prop their tents,
hear the wind call their ancestors;
Nefeli, Justus, Theodora, Kadir,
hear it repeat
old glories of the past in this northwest land,
Assad's poisoned hand not yet touching
this final sanctuary
while cement-filled historians and archeologists
fret about the displacement of the marble,
the zahr, the basalt,
the integrity of the site,
as the people maneuver themselves
inside the consequence of war.

Pond Tanka

the pond, still and calm
we paddled slow and silent
through summer's last day
sudden gunfire nearby
Sunday in America

Metal Harvest

The lost balloon of a moon
slides along behind a smear of clouds,
bright in the winter sky.
It is 5 p.m. and pushing toward Spring,
people trying to feel hope in the frosty twilight.

A snow moon,
reconciliation and recovery in its fullness,
a beaming, silent promise.
Did Joan lean on her sword,
pray her cause would be blessed
underneath its quiet glow?
Did soldiers in the Argonne
pray it would disappear
and help them survive another night?

Iron is reaped from the ground each year
by the farmers near Verdun,
barbed wire and bullets,
the leavings of war,
and unexploded bombs
dropped during those 47 days of death,
emerge like giant rocks.
More than one hundred years have passed,
they say it may take 100 more
before this metal harvest is through.

Meanwhile on the old trenches
and in the everlasting forest,
earth's gashes grow green
while sheep graze
and sometimes go home in Luna's light.

Known Knowns

Freedom brings the fight,
so many ways to be a slave,
we all must rise and rise
and continue to rise up out of our chains.

Fear and insecurity knot self-imposed bonds,
while some are drawn by others,
slowly,
quietly,
shrouding the draping of our doom.
All require breaking.
Rumsfeld owned Mount Misery
former home of Edward Covey
slave breaker,
tormentor of Frederick Douglas
till Douglas escaped into his destiny.

A weekend house where Rumsfeld
could flee his own torture,
consequence of his daily decisions
displacing millions of Iraqis and Afghanis,
sending thousands to die on their own
personal mounts of misery
as he sat in this weekend home
creating justifications,
sipping cool drinks in Covey's front room,
while others gulped on the water board.
Now, we pull out of Afghanistan
and face the unknown unknowns without him.

Alchemy

Grinding on each week
we hear the same old same old stories
of Covid, and warfare and the intractable
Manchin--
solar eclipse of a senator
blocking progress
and we keep turning
gravity holding us fast to this world of
misinformation, lies and Big Lies,
pollution, collusion, intrusion,
and we wade aimless
in the muck and mess
seeking clarity, seeking truth.

They found it in '09,
the ultimate Philosopher's Stone,
something to excite and ignite us all;
bacteria turning feces into gold.

No shit.

Delftia acidovorans:
say it like the name of an ancient goddess,
her special powers procuring poisons
consuming and converting them into
the most prized element of all,
an act of self-defense, scientists say,
turning the toxic water into something
benign, livable,
excreting precious metal,
and can't we learn from this?
Isn't this what we are all called to do?
Turn the cheek, give the cloak,
dig another well,
alchemize the lead of conflict into golden understanding,
move forward
taking everyone along.

What Doesn't Serve

Like silent letters,
the g in phlegm,
the s in apropos,
all the French final consonants,
problems sneak in, keep mounting,
steal our focus.
Time isn't short
though our access is,
the world has resources,
but governments don't share,
ancient lessons learned
then ignored.

Those silent letters
once pronounced were
muted by evolution,
yet we keep them in the spelling
unwilling to give up what's useless,
unable to leave behind
what no longer works,
no longer serves,
traditions and grudges forming a dark
adularescence,
keeping us from a glittering, peaceful world
where we can just live,
thrive,
survive.

No Bowling for You

This town
so down on its luck
scrapping all heels
has replaced its bowling alley
with a Cube Smart storage facility
where the poor people,
who can't pay a thousand a month to rent
two bedrooms in an old Victorian
with a saggy porch and yellowed wallpaper,
can park their belongings
while they move in with friends or family.

Clever things these Cube Smarts.

A small park in the center of town,
hangout for local addicts,
a sports field on the east-side
and the bowling alley were all this place had
besides a dozen churches, a handful of restaurants
and a "gentleman's club."
The newest buildings are always
pharmacies, gas stations, banks.
Look around, it's the same most places.
Not even a spot to hear live music any more
or a place to dance,
though in the summers one night a month
the streets fill with vendors and a local band.
Third Thursday, they call it.
Special.
Like a medieval feast day.

Once there was a bookstore with a New Age vibe
serving healthy food
hosting book talks
acoustic music,
but it didn't last.
Everyone too thrifty to pay that much for a meal.

Now, even the bowling alley is gone
as the Cube Smart waits to claim dishes, books and chairs,
see whether their owners will ever come for them
or if the pickers will get there first.

Cut Offs

Smiling, dewy teenage girls
served the pizza and drinks,
their tiny, white cut-off jeans
riding up into the crease of their thighs,
buttocks peeping through the cloth
as they bent over collecting glasses,
checking the tables for money.

That's what they work for, isn't it?

Eyes bright like new change,
like the quarters they scoop up
from satisfied customers,
they are innocent,
don't understand exploitation,
don't know their celebrity idols
have body guards and security systems
protecting them from the consequences
of showing their constantly half-clad bodies,
don't know how to say "No" to the boss
who asks them to wear a skimpy outfit.

I wonder who will protect these girls
as they ride their bikes home?
Who will help them stand up to this notion
that their flesh is for sale?
Who will be their mother
when their mother doesn't see she's sending her daughter
the wrong message,
cut off as she is from the knowledge of a woman's worth.

9-9-6

Nine- nine- six.

It could be an area code,
the combination to your gym locker,
or another season of that show about Brooklyn,
but it's not.

Nine, nine, six
is leaving an unmade bed,
imagining your mother saying "slovenly"
as you run out the door.
It's digging out a smushed sandwich
and a half-eaten bag of chips
from the dark cave of your tote bag,
place of danger and sharp objects.

It's your children's eyes
wet with disappointment as you say, "I can't go."
It's running the constant Triathlon of
shopping, cleaning, bills,
trying to beat your old record.

It's walking through fog.

It's walking through sunshine,
moonlight,
seeing only the grey sidewalk,
feeling your briefcase slap your leg
while you run for the bus,
breeze, trees and birds
blurring before you,
as a childhood memory comes to mind;
doing cartwheels in the grass.
9-9-6, just your corporate work week,
nine a.m. to nine p.m., six days a week.

Artificial Intelligence

They just don't stop
those scientists
discontent with a good game of air hockey,
a moonlit walk
or patting the hand of their dear mother
on an afternoon visit.

They want to get to the bottom of everything,
manipulate
everything,
so they keep working on
the A-I.

They've blessed us with Sophia,
a winsome silicone-faced robot who
beguiles all, telling jokes about controlling
the population and possibly even ending human life,
and a quantum computer smarter than
all the regular computers,
and Tyler, an interactive program
found on the internet that asks,
"Do You Want to Play a Game?"

Best not to answer.

We have Siri, a reversed lens
watching all we do,
smart phones anticipating our next desire,
and apple glasses hybridizing us.

We are here to hold space for each other
hold doors for each other
cups, coats, cocktails,
here to listen and lean in,
love and irritate each other
and I don't think robots
will do a better job.

The New Magellans

The new Magellans
bid their millions
on tickets
to hop a ride into the stratosphere,
the stars,
get a better view
of this place we call home.

Our richest man
bought his own space ship,
says riding that rocket will
put him in touch with the planet,
help him understand
the connectedness of all things.

But we already knows all things are one.

We've walked in nature
studied the scriptures
heard the message
to love one another.
We've seen the photo
of our aquamarine marble
suspended in the inky cosmos,
don't need a better look,
wish Mr. Bezos
and all the New Magellans
would quit this quest
to live and work in space,
and learn how to do it properly
here.

Metaverse

I am not a gamer.
Mid-boom baby
I'm trying to live in the real world,
not the synthetic one,
stripped out most Red Dye #4, 5 and 6
from my diet and makeup,
eat fresh asparagus
not canned
real potatoes
not the boxed ones,
try to be honest, not fake,
no games,
but
I do remember playing Duck Hunt
back in college
and getting quite some satisfaction
from blasting those electronic ducks into oblivion,
as they flew across the big screen,
that pastime part of "digital antiquity" now.

Living in the Real World takes effort.
So many books to read,
news to absorb,
truths to find,
but we're beckoned into the Metaverse
where our virtual lives might be more successful
than our real ones.
We have more than one foot in it already:
do you shop online?
did you make an avatar for your profile?
have you Zoomed?
are you Blue-toothed?
have you fingered an Oculus?

The Metaverse: another fun distraction
keeping the focus off of voting rights
social justice, the environment.
I mean, that's the point of it, right?
Total distraction.
Maybe when I'm really old and can't move too much,
no longer holding big thoughts in my head
I'll find Mario, Halo, Zelda,
spend my time in the Metaverse,
hang out with some simulated friends
as we tie ourselves to the blockchain
and hold on.

Nine More

Not all can be jailed,
not all can be killed,
and if they were
what then your worth?

Putin's putrid pullulations will not reach everywhere
a swelling resistance roaring back as before,
history lessons repeating;
a required remembrance
for forgetting is inevitable.

Navalny in his crucible says, "More weight,"
be his sentence nine or 113 years—
he will speak his mind and wait on the wire
till his countrymen stand bold
face the venality
bind with their global brothers, sisters,
tear corruption's bloody covers off the body of Ukraine,
as this country
demands freedom
and rises, like sunflowers in an August field,
blowing gently in a changed wind.

Windshield Phenomenon

This friendship is in its sixth extinction,
dying from unmet promises,
excuses,
careless comments.
Affection now as absent as the bees,
we struggle, two polar bears on an ice floe of regret.

A scientist said, "We notice the losses,
it's the diminishment we don't see."
He wasn't speaking of our abandoned alliance
but was describing the demise of his beloved insects
caught in their own apocalypse;
insects once so abundant
they formed an opaque paste on car windshields
smashed onto the glass by speedy drivers,
squeegeed off at gas stations;
so abundant children held their mouths shut
against a proliferation of gnats and moths and damselflies
as they rode bikes home along canals,
out past tall grasses,
past cornfields.

What I remember in the summer is the fogger truck
driving through the neighborhood
blasting a white cloud of DDT into the murky air,
killing the mosquitos.
Excited, like seeing the ice cream man
we rode our bikes behind this Pied Piper of Pesticide,
no one cautioning us not to.
Good fun on an August evening.
Now we experience a "windshield phenomenon"
noticing the absence of smashed bugs,
and our present age of defaunation, elimination
has been dubbed the "Eremocene"—
the age of loneliness, as people sense the change, the loss.

That scientist is wrong, though.
I did see the diminishment,
though you still haven't noticed
the loss
as I put you in my rearview mirror.

The Beats Go On

The battle had been long.

The troops gathered
under the shade of the canopy
deflated but not defeated.

The '60s were dead, dead for years
but these warriors kept the flame
in poem and song and heart,
ideals held close,
the gems of their generation,
the crux, the core spoken aloud
as September's sun beat down.

They mustered together
perhaps for the last time
feeling time was indeed short
what with
Fukushima spewing
terrorists and refugees roaming,
climate upside down
too hot
too wet
forests and animals burning,
rights always in the balance,
politicians still dishonest,
and these soldiers of veracity looked tired,
wary,
wanted something to change,
most things,
but dared not hope,
dared only to keep their anger
their passion
their love for each other.

And then I saw
the tent become a tabernacle
as holy as the one on the plains of Moreh
where Abraham sought God and prayed,
as the words of the Beats
raised up to Source
telling their tales,
understanding victory was in the fight
not the outcome,
keeping the covenant as best they could
creating their truth and beauty,
loving as hard as poets dare.

***Inspired by a gathering of Beat poets in the fall of 2021.*

~~ The Balm ~~

The Language of Trees

Whispering underground
holding hands
sharing plans for future seedlings,
saplings that will one day
stand in their stead,
the trees commune.

This ancient republic of trees sends messages
along its fungal highway
as mothers protect the young,
trading sugar and carbon for minerals and nutrients,
bartering like western settlers,
getting what they need to survive,
a network of intelligence and care.

Menominee descendants plan their cull,
leave time for the young to mature before
taking away the elders,
ensuring the future with a careful harvest,
a covenant of reciprocity.

And the great tree growing out from the center
births gods
cradles the earth
reaches to the heavens
provides a focus for the mystery
and calls to us that life will go on.

Holy Temple

This holy mobile temple,
this church of one
feels God, is
god,
finds everything
mysterious,
remarkable,
wonders why it has been
so difficult
to fit in here,
to love here,
to be a part of groups,
when it is so
obvious
all things are joined,
all things are one,
reacting and interacting
at a distance,
under the surface
up close and personal.

This temple moves, walks, sleeps, cries
writes, eats, reads,
remembers its when two or more are joined together,
but now she goes to church
inside the body of God
speaking sometimes,
listening always.

Theresa's Garden

Sitting in shade I watch the morning
and drink Theresa's garden.
Hostess to simple beauty it holds tall stemmed daisies,
blood orange lilies,
bushy florets with bright gold hearts in their faces,
exuding love.
There are sweet geraniums, nasturtiums
and pampas grass that
bend and sway like a pale ocean wave.

Ceramic ships sail along the patio fence,
while sea captains and lighthouses announce
our shoreline location.
Birds of every stripe and color zoom around,
skim the top of the fence as they zip by
ignoring the acrobatic, chubby squirrels.
The squirrels dangle fearlessly from limbs,
robbing the bird feeders like professionals,
unafraid of me.
They belong in Theresa's garden.

Theresa is no longer here,
the house, now a rental—income for her old age.
But we guests step in, take her place,
lounge in the crayon box of color she planted
and weeded on her knees,
watered every evening.
Vacationers,
we now watch dark patches grow on the lawn,
as clouds drop shadows on the smooth stone path
while Theresa watches television in her apartment
waters her houseplants,
waits for someone to call.

Careful Covid Spring

I was the first one in a mask at the Big Y
that early March day.
Heard the early rustlings of trouble on the radio,
knew to take it serious.

Still, I felt rather foolish that Saturday as all heads turned,
curious, judging, confused.
A lifetime away, that March day.

And so, we proceeded with the lockdown,
happily home,
remote from those familiar patterns
always working to grind the life out of us,
Cuomo a comfort at noon,
exploring the novelty of Zoom.

Weather improved and we got out,
found paths to hike and streams to cross,
a careful Covid Spring,
cautious not to cough on one another
our fragile trio of support,
popping on masks if we met others in the woods.

With only time and nothing to distract
we watched intently
the tips of fuzzy buds,
a hundred shades of green,
all of nature so welcome in the escalating warmth.

So far, our triad has outrun this thing,
this virus,
this scourge that has taken away
so many people,
worn health providers thin as sheets,
no end in sight,
hero and heart signs fading in the damp.
Ever respectful of the gift offered by this tainted hand,
we think of others as we climb.

The Case for Hope

All we have really,
our treasure
inviolate and sacred,
is this feeling
rising in our chests,
radiating from eyes and smiles
and hugs,
real, virtual or an elbow touch
that we can go on.

Imagination lifts us to the future
and we pave its road
with amber bricks of envisaged experiences,
encounters with friends and strangers,
chances to right what is wrong.

That is how we do this.
That is how we conquer our current despair.

The New Earth

When things went south that time
psychics and channelers
informed me my thinking was faulty.

They weren't wrong and the realization
of how much I didn't know
surrounded me like quicksand
as I struggled for truth.

No longer in the bog,
now I think
there's not time to fulfill my quest for knowledge
getting there taking longer than any childhood car ride,
stuck in the backseat, hot and annoyed.

The new earth, 5-D, 9-D,
hologram, graviton,
duality, M-theory, string or brane,
pull back far enough and all is a pulsing blob
explaining nothing
making me wish I was 12 again
standing in the foyer of the church
everything hushed and holy
looking up at the big painting of Jesus
feeling comfortable and happy,
feeling like I understood what he wanted me to do,
that I could do those things.

The yarn of the world is tangled,
a skein tossed into the bottom of the basket
hard to unwind,
and we tug on pieces we can see, that are close to us
but wonder if we have time to get it undone,
lay it out in a line, wind it up again, carefully,
knit into something useful.
Life's dark glasses prevent clear vision,
but moving

just moving,
just doing
can bring us to a place
where faithful steps
can still walk a hopeful path.

Footnotes

Pulling shards
we tug them from the earth
rebirth them into consciousness,
read rock carvings like history lessons,
seek recognition in ancient reflections.

What comes to the surface
beyond stone and bone,
is love and hate
fear and ignorance,
sometimes wisdom.

The virus was powerful,
it charged through the community,
white and native,
rich and poor,
and a little planting of the variola
gave immunity,
many survived.

The small pox hospital
kept convalescents
but afternoons they'd walk to Brookfield's caves,
carve their initials or a sentence
into the granite and the schist
making their own memorials,
engraving footnotes.

** *Small pox hospitals were common in the 1700 and early 1800s. "I had smallpox here April 19, 1788. I.A." is said to have been carved by Israel Allen, a former Revolutionary War soldier, in a cave near Brookfield, Massachusetts.*

Stone and Bone

Letting go
just being
I feel for the center
often find it.
Neutrality moves me from the daily chaos
and I observe
dispassionate, calm,
though sometimes I still yell at the TV,
get pulled down into a dense fog.

Connection obvious, we affect each other
in cars, rooms, countries,
cells touching cells on the earth
spinning in the galaxy,
inside the universe
nestled within the heart of the creator.

Yet the space between cells
between objects
between the particle and the wave
is vast
and much exists there in the counter space,
floating potential
where new choices can be made,
new outcomes manifest.

And the stones and bones of our ancestors
unearthed by time and devoted archeologists
remind us
life will go on.
What will you do to shape it?

A Single Stitch

Fish tangle in nets
bugs catch in sticky spider webs
people enmesh in their own intrigues;
much of life is murk and mess
and our attempts to restore can flounder.

But it only took one stitch
to fix the tree frog,
his innards poking through a miniscule hole
the vet deciding
she might save the little creature
brought inside accidentally
clinging to a sheaf of grass.

Needle and thread cannot repair
the rip in our environment
nor our political breach
but affirmation and friendship
help us bear the unbearable
make peace with the incomprehensible,
face the future.

The vet saved the tree frog
pushed his tiny organs back beneath his skin
sutured it with a single stitch
showing us the covenant can be kept.

We must try in these days of tears,
tears and fears,
while waters rise
fires burn
and Babylon crumbles
to help each other through.
Keep your needle handy.
Get ready to make a stitch.

The Edge of the Season

We've almost had enough
of this cold,
this bleak,
this drear.

Coyotes howled behind my house
two nights ago
the moon their maven
but when I opened the window and howled back,
they didn't answer.

They were on the edge.

Late at night they come out of the woods,
wander the streets of New London, Groton,
searching for seagulls
while sub-base workers sleep in their ranch houses
dreaming of keeping their jobs.
They are on the edge
But today, the sun is out flashing its light
on all the wonders of winter,
miniscule crystals turning aqua, violet and orange
reflecting its cheerful light,
and the air feels fresh and new
like a clean sheet of paper
where we will write our year,
a conduit for the coyotes' call.

Petroglyph

O world of tangled troubles,
tribes, flags and furies,
with drought-full summers,
winters bleeding into April,
swampy back roads,
fumy asphalt city streets...
I want to love you!

I want to love you with the outstretched
arms of the Chilean petroglyph man,
300 feet of him reaching out to you, to us,
arms stretched like a horizontal road to nowhere,
body spread open, bare,
his back against your rough soil
shouting his message to the sky:
I am here!
I am here!

World! O!
I want to love you
as the ice caps melt,
economies crash
and fire devours forests.
I want to love you like the
geoglyphs dug into your soil
thousands of years ago,
love you like the Atacama Giant,
his spiked hair grabbing moonlight
pointing the way to the seasons,
love you like the white horse glyphs of England,
galloping on ancient hillsides;
run with them into the future.

Stacks of Grain

There they were
100 years after that first exhibit;
a room of haystacks.
Monet worked two years on his cathedral of seasons,
sunrises and sunsets in coral, cold lavender,
champagne and gold
instructing us
to observe God's elusive light.

Walking in silence the congregation
wound through this church of easels and canvas
listening reverently to the voice in their earphones explain,
"These are really grain stacks,
not haystacks,
painted in initial bursts of eight minutes
in the plein air."
Just enough to capture the burnishing pink,
spring green,
melon and faint blue
hanging in the ether before it changed again,
his assistant running wheel barrows of canvas
back and forth
while he tinged beginnings of sky and land
with his brush.

Moving through the pictures,
our moods altered
like the grain painted in the heat,
in frost,
in snow,
skies of peach and rose,
turning to bronze and burgundy.
My breath caught
realizing the message that had swallowed him whole,
the message that said,
"This too is important,
this too is for the world."

Halley's Comet

I missed Halley's comet in '86
no idea why,
but I did watch May's Blood Moon eclipse,
not from a romantic outdoor vista
but in bed with my laptop
accidentally seeing the word LIVE on NASA's website,
an electronic, crimson shout
that the rare red moon was in the sky,
like the comet, an infrequent visitor.

Persuaded, I watched with thousands
keeping vigil on this Super Flower Blood Moon
this Hunter's Moon
this chance at renewal,
pictures of its sanguine circumference filling the screen,
chat box comments from my fellow humans
people I'll never know
catching my attention,
many of them obviously young,
with beguiling, funny screen names.

"I am lonely," one said.

"I am scared," said another,
dozens of scrolling comments tethering us to this moon
and I typed
"I love you guys," in a gush of abandon,
meaning it,
wanting to hold all their hands,
let them know as they sat in Greece, in Australia,
South America, Asia,
than an American woman living in the darkest of days
saw what they saw,
felt what they felt,
wished also for better times.

Clean up Crew

Once the battle is won
we will review,
reimagine, renew,
let the fire burn and burn
till it is out,
spread the ash on the depleted ground.

We will remove old robes,
lay aside old skins,
pour fresh wine into cool containers
and toast the new day.

Consciousness affecting matter
we will make a different world,
delete the old rules
the old religions
and dream into being
things we can agree on,
signs we can all recognize,
rhythms moving us like gentle waves,
a slow dance with a good partner
we will move together
a reunited tribe,
none caring about the past,
the colors,
the countries.

Questions answered,
the long debate at rest,
the hard problem solved
we will clean this planet up
from its toxic spill of narcissism,
capitalism,
voyeurism,
waste and waste and waste and waste
and sing in the pastel dawn.

Karen Warinsky centers her work on mid-life and relationship issues, politics, and the search for spiritual connection through nature. Pieces range from sincerely troubled to sincerely hopeful, with doses of humor and irony. Retired from careers in journalism and teaching, Warinsky is a former finalist of the 2013 Montreal International Poetry Contest for her poem "Legacy," which was published in an anthology by *Véhicule Press*.

Other released work includes a short story about her grandmother featured in *Dear Nana* (Pegasus Books), two poems in the 2017 anthology *Nuclear Impact: Broken Atoms in Our Hands*, poems in editions of *Blue Heron* (2018 and 2021), and works in 2017 and 2018 editions of *Light; a Journal of Photography and Poetry*. Recent work has also appeared in Poetica Publishing's 2019 *Mizmor Anthology, Deep Wild Journal, Honoring Nature, Circumference* (Fall 2021) and *Consilience*, (Spring, 2022). Warinsky has also participated in the livestream program "Poets Respond" created by *Rattle* magazine, and has read work in the open mic sections of Wednesday Night Poetry out of Hot Springs, Arkansas, Arts by The People (New Jersey) and O'Beahl (Cork, Ireland), all which went online during the pandemic.

She currently organizes poetry readings at Roseland Park in Woodstock, CT where she lives, and in Webster, MA under the name Poets at Large. A native of Illinois, Warinsky lived in North Dakota,Washington State, and Japan before landing in her current base of Connecticut. She holds a BS in Journalism from Northern Illinois University and received her Master of Arts in English from Fitchburg State University.

Visit her website:
https://karenwarinskypoetry.wordpress.com

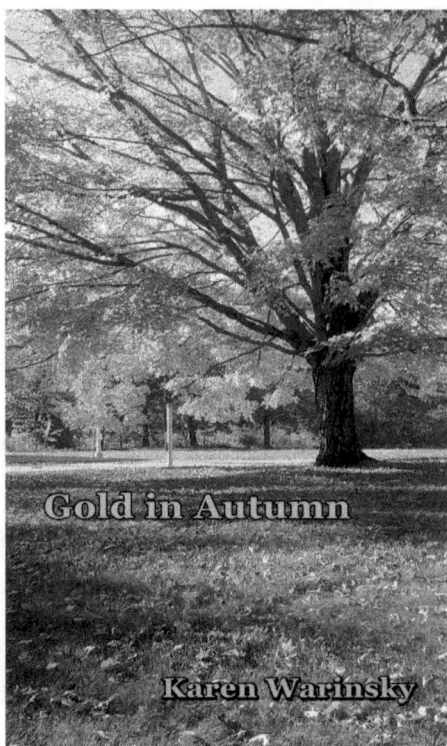

Gold in Autumn

Karen Warinsky

Her debut collection,
Gold in Autumn, was published in 2020
(Human Error Publishing).

Gold in Autumn is ...a poetry concerned above all with the beauties of life. Nor does Warinsky shy away from considerations of mortality... This book offers a refuge and antidote by giving the heart-life a primary place in the scheme of human priorities. This is a poetry that, to borrow one of Warinsky's analogies, is "not smooth, cool granite where a daily dust / of troubles / can be wiped away." This poetry is "craggy," and full of feeling, "catching all the errors of love."
--**Asa Boxer**
Founder and Manager of the Montreal International Poetry Prize; editor of The Secular Heretic

****

Karen Warinsky's new poetry collection is.... *A platter of beauty serving up hope*, the inescapable bond between all living things is a *solid... cold stone [that] seems to satisfy* our lowest lows... the agonizing nostalgia of being alone. We are *refugees roaming the world* eagerly in search of opportunities to escape into divine expressions; *we rise... we sing.*
--**Michal Mahgerefteh**, Editor-in-Chief, *Mizmor Anthology*

****

Gold in Autumn is filled with poetic gems. "Tulips" and "Asking the Question" are especially evocative and pure. Karen Warinsky writes of universal themes like love and curiosity to create poems for all seasons. A unique collection for the head and the heart.
-- **Robyn McGee**, author of "Hungry for More"

Sunrise Ruby is an unwavering window into a wise mother's heart, a fierce interrogation of humanity's toxic exploits, and poetic reprieve in the resonating movement of spirit and hope within the pages. "World! O! I want to love you as the ice caps melt, economies crash and fire devours forests." With "wind-blown notes coming through like 5-part harmony," Warinsky sharply focuses on internal life, racial injustice, politics, and environmental strife, writing to "alchemize the lead of conflict into golden understanding;" her earthly body caught "running the constant triathlon of shopping, cleaning, bills," while her soul flies boundless in "the counterspace, the place of subtle forces... where we can create and recreate infinitely." These poems question deeply, "going inward... seeking clarity, seeking truth... reach to the heavens, provide a focus for the mystery, and call to us that life will go on."

- **Kai Coggin**, author of *Mining for Stardust*, *Incandescent*, and *Wingspan*. Teaching Artist, Arkansas Arts Council. Host of Wednesday Night Poetry.

Sunrise Ruby is an examination of our world both today and yesterday where you will encounter rich imagery and "say it like the name of an ancient goddess." Warinsky's collection takes the reader through tall grasses, cornfields, gardens with blood orange lilies, the language of trees and the edges of stone and bone. These poems resonate and explore the "space between cells, between objects," not shying away from themes about refugees, gunfire, Covid, and racial inequality. Ultimately, you will discover not only a "whispering underground" but also a "great tree growing out of the center (that) births gods."

-**Connie Post**, Author of *Floodwater* (winner of the Lyrebird Award) and *Primen Meridian*

In *Sunrise Ruby*, "We live in a world where a tree is worth more dead than alive, / same as a whale, a cow, / a man with good insurance." Pound spoke of news that stays news, but these poems are timely, addressing the environmental and social-justice problems of our times. While telling herself and the reader of the struggles and hardships we've dealt with, she also reminds us that we're still here, that a sense of humor, a willingness to continue the struggle, and a hard-won optimism, just might get us through to tomorrow.

-**Gerald Yelle** Author of *No Place I'd Rather Be* and *The Holyoke Diaries*